SO SMALL A POCKET

POEMS by

Mary Plutchak

PHOTOGRAPHS by

Dan Plutchak

CARROUSEL PRESS

1991

Grateful acknowledgement is made to the following publications in which some of these poems first appeared:

VIEW
FOXFIRE
PRAIRIE POET
GRIT

Library of Congress Catalog
Card Number 91-73395

ISBN 0-9630322-0-8

Carrousel Press, 1605 Sullivan Ave., Kaukauna, Wisconsin 54130

Look back on time with kindly eyes,
　　He doubtless did his best;
How softly sinks his trembling sun,
　　In human nature's west!

EMILY DICKINSON

For Mother

CONTENTS

III. FROM THE WINGS

I noticed the A in Rialto was missing. Did Poppa know? I walked around the back alley to the stage door. No one was around. The door gave way to my touch. It had seemed so heavy when I was little. Such an impenetrable barrier between my two worlds of growing up. Outside the door Momma, school, starched dresses; inside Poppa, dancing lessons, pink tutus, and shiny black tap shoes.

I found the light switch. The stage had the early morning look of a woman before make-up and getting organized. I walked across the dusty darkening floorboards pausing to touch the old familiar pulleys and ropes that held the lights, curtains, and backdrops high above the stage. Loosened they could turn it into a country garden, a medieval dungeon or a plank, Thorton Wilder-like, could be a soda fountain. This the most make believe of all the making believe, the pretense of not pretending.

Without the props and artifacts, this was the way I best remembered the stage, comfortable and waiting to appear to be whatever it was decided it should appear to be.

How do we decide things?

I sank into an ancient armchair in the wings and stared at the empty stage. I remembered Saturday mornings so diligently practicing the "Big Apple" with all the awkwardness of adolescence, then on to the solemnity of church, practicing, "I Am a Soldier of the Lord". The show on Saturday night; confirmation on Sunday morning. Which was the reality? Which the illusion? How did they fit together?

And even earlier than that when I was eight. We hadn't been told before how we would appear. I only knew the flesh colored leotard itched. Dancing behind pink chiffon, the rose colored footlights rendered us nude imps for an audience that could snicker at naked awkward little girls or see the poetry of beguiling innocence. You pick your illusion. When it was over we were told how we had appeared and were expected to share in the delight of a successful illusion. I remember feeling only willfully indignant. Never, no never again, would I be used unwittingly to create for others, any others, the illusions they needed to feed on.

I had thought I could be like Blackstone creating my own illusions, the appearance of smooth magic, out of props, dexterity, and the most mundane of logic. As long as I knew, in my secret self where the latch was hidden that caused the seamless box to give way I could live any fantasy.

Have I been dishonest? The only honesty I know is to protect the center of me inside the fairy tale of living out a life. The center of me must admit to whatever illusion I'm creating.

Or is reality created by artistry?

I remember Karl the Juggler keeping all those colored spheres in motion, segmented and whirling in space. It was easy to make the mistake of thinking that somehow the motion and the centrifugal force kept the spheres from falling. Or you might have decided the measured systematic movement of the juggler's wrists keep them all in space. But see his feet firmly planted on the stage? When he decides he's had enough the wrists will stop, the spheres will falter, careening recklessly through space. Karl may or may not catch them. But when *he* wills it, his heels will click together and he'll bow to the applause. His trick is done. The colored worlds are packed away.

What happens now? I looked up at the faded maroon curtains waiting to be lowered for another time. I looked at the empty stage and it was waiting, too. Not demanding a role, just waiting.

I sat there stripped of all the props and settings of my life. The only artifacts, the experiences that had thus far shaped my life knotted together like the colored handkerchiefs Blackstone could pull out of his small breast pocket. Now red and green and gold and blue. Endlessly they came out of that pocket while the orchestra played the suspense. And when you knew it had no end -- it ended.

The magic was not infinity after all, but only that so many knotted handkerchiefs could come out of so small a pocket.

I. ENTER LEFT

11

ABOUT KIDS AND HILLS

Kids
run up hills
and roll
down
then stop
grow up
and need
reasons.

The cranium
splits.

Both ways
were fun,
the run up
and the tumble
down.

We built
bulldozers
that ate
the hill.

There was a
reason
for that.

One reason -- one hill.

More kids found
more hills
until
we found more reasons.

As a kid
I understood
about running
and rolling down.
It was a kid thing
we did.

I didn't understand
Humpty Dumpty
or Jack and Jill.

Silly and obtuse

sit still and listen

a large person
spouting nonsense
before we slept.

GROWING GIRL

I spoiled the game
you said.
Without someone
to tie to the tree
no one could play
or have any fun.

How could there be
a rescuer
or three bad guys
if no one was
tied to the tree?

"It's my rope," I said,
"couldn't we jump
or have a
tug of war?"

"No way,
jumping is for sissies.
Who'd take a
girl on their side
for a tug of war?"

I took the length
of clothesline
back to mother.
I cut out paper dolls
alone. I wandered
in the woods
and learned
to jump the creek
and climb the trees.

I haven't cared much since
if you are having fun.

CAROLINE AT TWILIGHT

My epileptic child
beats her head
hard on the floor
to dissipate
her private aura.

Church bells plead
for services
evensong is heard
the heavy thud
on summer porches
evening paper
satiate and swelling
glut of bloody truths.

Caroline does not
simply endure
beyond her aura now
she is painting me a picture
full of flowers.

A SHIELD

Today is dressed
in light and giddy green
before the lush fulfillment
of its promise.

Yesterday
that wept
in icy corners
hiding from the wind
is blown away.

I warn tomorrow
with its sway
to twist and torture promise
not to prey.

I hold today
tightfisted
like a shield
before its face.

MORNING IN CHICAGO

The elevated train screeched
high above the sooty street.
Night workers struggled
to remain awake
the last swaying mile.

Dull eyed paper venders
and queasy stomached managers
of glossy six story emporiums
checked their wares
against the coming day.

The windswept sluggish river churned.

The sun rose bravely to bestow
its clouded blessing.

All was ready
to receive
a bus load of tidy children
from the suburbs
who were too excited to eat breakfast and
had never been to the museum.

BEFORE THE ELEGY

A somber sense of waiting
hushed the room
gloom like disembodied dust
in shafts of sun
flecked
settled quiet over everything.
Strangers murmured
in the wake of waiting.

Hothouse mums and marigolds
released
a lying scent
not strong enough to contradict
the truth of ending.

AFTER THE RAIN

Carrie and I
walked through
the diesel air
to where
eight small lilies of
the valley grew.

Holding that bit of
freshness to her face
her hand in mine
we crossed the bridge halfway
to watch
the water
rain lifted now
above the slimy rock.

One dead carp his belly up
was thrust in motion
by the swirling of detergent foam.

Squeezing my hand
she squealed, "Look Mommie,
fishes swimming."
Her eyes sought mine
to share the wonder.

SURFACE OF A MIRROR

Skipping stones in the water
jumping off a swing
tree top high
I don't anymore.

I drive to teas
in the sunny seasons.
Collecting driftwood
is permissible.

This year
I accidentally cracked
the surface of a mirror.
I'll find
the kind of stones that skip.

MARCH

I feel the painful possibility
of spring.
The hard packed snow, the ice
are turned to fluid motion
by a sun
gone sweet in solace.

When winter came
I thought I could not live
within a world gone cold
but now
I'm frightened more
by the warm
possibility of spring.

TEMPTATION

I would like to
sit on a cloud
in a clear sky
serene as a Buddha.

Below me the wind,
rain, fingers making
mud pies and a manly
tortoise inching.

Never to tumble
howling from the sky
in wind and rain
to fashion pots of clay
or wait in the turtle's path.

I'd much prefer
to sit in timeless
empty clarity
serene as sin.

II. STAGE RIGHT

MOTHER'S DAY

Scented soaps
in flowered wrappers
a sachet for
my nightie drawer.

I remember large
white bars of ivory
soaping up your tummies,
squeals of delight,
lifting you
dripping and squirming
toweled down
bedded in warm flannel.

Who do you see?
A woman in need
of scented soaps and sachets?

Do you remember me
bending down
up to my elbows
in babies and bath water?

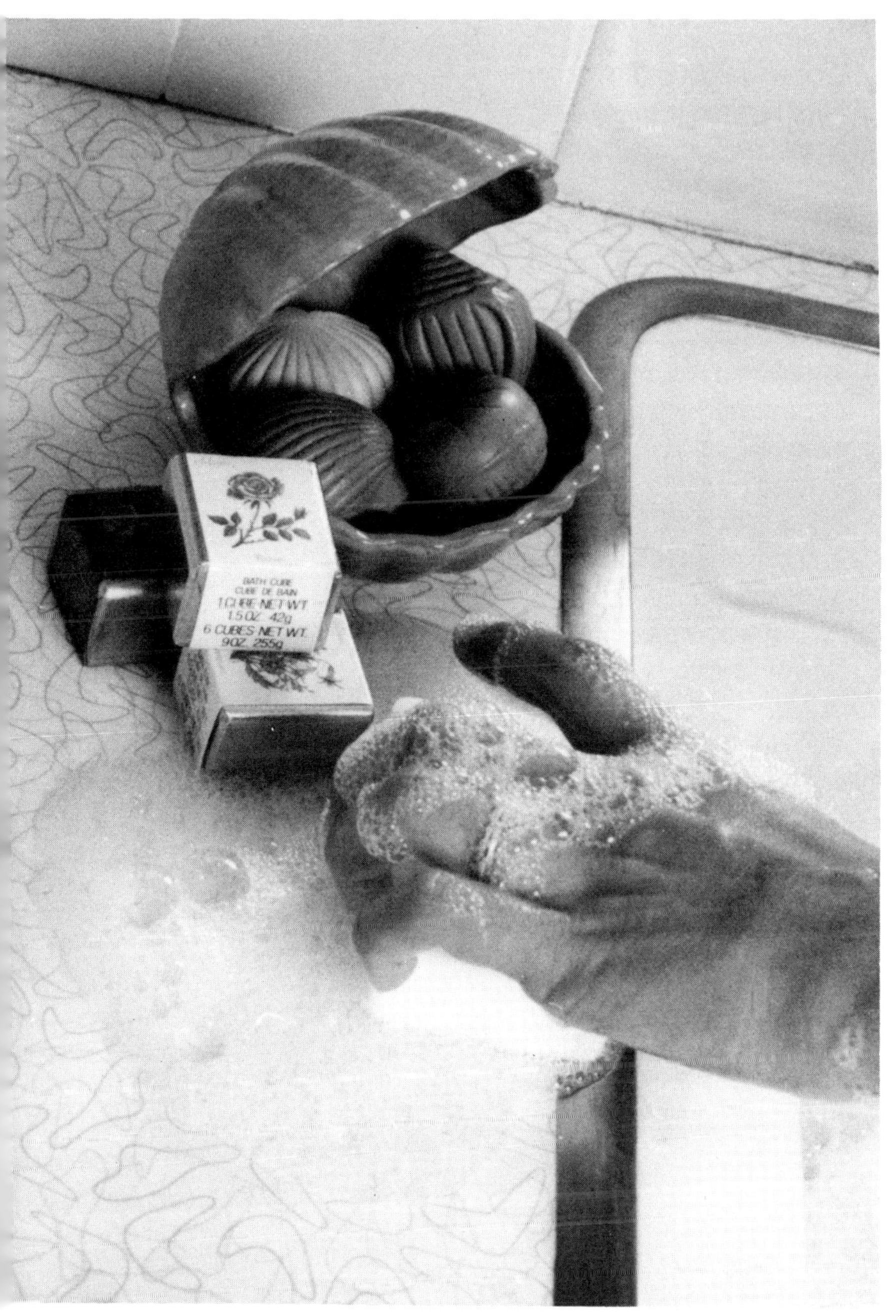

BATH CUBE
CUBE DE BAIN
1 CUBE NET WT.
1.5 OZ. 42g
6 CUBES NET WT.
9 OZ. 255g

I IMAGINE MYSELF

I imagine myself
litho and winsome,
wonderful and wise.

I tried new clothes,
and make-up on my eyes,
sucking in my belly,
but the mirror never lied.

I am not young, or beautiful,
or even, heaven help me,
strikingly alive!
A little like the other
round and robust mothers
who despise
their drooping eyelids
and their sagging thighs.

I cried
as flesh and mirror
did devise
a vision poorly sized.

I stared and eyed,
then flung a hairbrush
at the image
mirror and flesh contrived!

Enough! Denied!

I sally forth to court
the inner eye.

And fortified,

I imagine myself
lithe and winsome
wonderful and wise.

ONLY THE SMALL SNAKES BELONG

Lost somewhere
in other people's lives.
Locked in.
Hunting through
others' basements
for the souvenirs
I wouldn't recognize,
even if I found
them.

This basement has
only a back door,
like a cave
found in a hill.

Enter from sweet
tall grass
overgrown
hiding an occasional
small snake.

There is no light.

When the sun shines
it chooses
the deep lagoon
beyond the grass.

The lagoon is
city property;
the house rented.

Only the small snakes
belong,
prodded by twigs
held by children.

DESTINY

Some say
destiny
catches up with you.

Like dirty dishes
in the sink,
standing in the way
of starting on
another day?

GLORIA MURIEL IS BOTHERED

Gloria Muriel
is bothered.
She hadn't imagined
she would be
so ordinary.

In bed
her head is barely
visible.
Her pelvis tight
against the sheets
for safety.

She imagines
a great green place
like forests from
old
Tarzan movies.

Sensations from
old
childhood dreams,
exotic -- fleet of foot
in a world of green.

Gloria Muriel flat
against the mattress
dreams --
these remomberings
from forests never
seen -- are quite
enough -- she
sleeps.

They named her
Gloria Muriel
not knowing
how ordinary
she would be.

MILD WINTER

This season
it hasn't been cold.
Commentators say
temperatures steady
even.

How erratic
this lack of blizzards,
below zero
home huddling
depression.

Not storm tossed
lost on country roads,
stalled on freeways,
fretting in airports.

We come and go
in ordinary clothes.
No plans frantically
changed. A day
arranged and simply
done.

The energy flows
hope does not
get buried in
so deep
that only spring
can thaw the bones.

Capricious gods
like to remind us
on occasion
our usual awful
expectations
are a myth
ordinariness
a great
a glorious gift.

GLORIA'S DELUSION

Gloria felt the water
licking at her ankles
before she saw it rise.

She knew about flood plains.
She built here anyway.
Didn't many others?

The view of the sea
the evening spray
was worth the risk

until the floods began.

The others she discovered
never believed
it would rise this high.

How could so many be
such fools and settle here
if the threat was real?

Some will build again
after telling each other
it wasn't so bad
and won't happen twice.

Gloria won't.

COFFEE WITH COUSIN SALLY

Cousin Sally was a knock-out.
Grew up believing
there was power in that.
Giggling and mincing
stroking a herringbone sleeve
looking up through lashes
stroked with black
mascara.

Her flat reminds.
Behind the dusty pictures
of the distant kids
pressed roses
doomed to dust
a dream
of spiral stairs.

Instead she had
laundry
mountains of it.
Sticky little hands
endless readings
of romance.

Over coffee of
regret -- the tale
of men not met --
bad luck -- the looks
a waste -- the bitter
taste of never was
a time when fate
fulfilled
the promise
of that mirrored face.

MRS. MEEGER'S COMING OUT

Mrs. Meeger
is starting a drive
to eliminate
booze, cigarettes and abortions
in our town.

This is the year
she's been waiting for.
All her life
she's hated
people playing,
drinking, smoking, dancing.

Stuck with too many babies
in the old tall house
on the corner;
home to generations
of her husband's family.

Sucked into
too much laundry,
too many streaked linoleum floors
children scurrying across
like micc
around her feet.

All gone now
except Mrs. Meeger
in the tall house
too much space
and faded paper walls.

"You made your bed
now lie in it", she's said
to the scurrying kids
who fled.

She would
eliminate substance abuse,
create a smoke free town,
and tear the clinic down.

Everyone said it was
the thing to do.
She'd waited and hated
in the old tall house.
This is her year.

TEMPO

Tempo is everything!

Life
      games
birdsongs
       dancing?

Do you need:
      lines on a poster
      Confucius says
      the golden mean?

Try
 tempo is everything!

Beats jogging.

HAPPY BIRTHDAY, TO ME!

I wrote
three poems today
in quick succession
like a triple orgasm.

Should I
rest
or risk, feeling
heavy eyelids
and the pencil
slip,
a go for four?

So there
one more!

TEA TIME

Tea time
and temperance
two tipsy teetotalers
and Terrance
trying their patience.

The tempest in the
teapot
is elderberry.
Slipped in by Terrance.

He visits his
grandfather's sisters
once every summer.

They look forward
to it.

HESTER'S VOICES

My cousin Hester
has four voices

Conspiratorial whispers I
remember best
and longest.
Her cheerleader
developed early.
Stern Mom
came later.

Lately as we
sit and chat
I hear
a tsk-tsk-tsk.

I think she should
get rid of that.

III. FROM THE WINGS

ARGYLE SOCKS

I wanted
argyle socks,
a store bought hat
with ribbons down the back,
a queen Anne desk,
or
no more
diapers on the line.

I wanted.

Now,
I remember best
a beach in twilight rain,
roller skating down a city hill,
night conversations on a
dusty step,
a lonely afternoon,
the distant high note
of a flute.

A GAMBLE

It's always a gamble
shiny stylish
the fit feels good
in the store
before the mirror
on the floor.

Will they walk
miles without blisters?
Guard against rain?
Match forgotten
skirts in the back
of the closet?

Or will this pair
after a try or two
join the other
not quite right
out of sight
gathering dust?
Always a gamble.

EVERGREEN

A slate grey sky robs
color from the trees,
stark black,
I need to close my eyes
imagining the green.

My back is to the
window now.
It is no accident
this room is painted blue.

I'll stay inside today
arranging flowers
touching the green stems
forgetting
forgetting
forgetting
the black tree
at my back.

WHICH TRUTH

Tenderly tracing
the blue vein
on the back of my hand
you breathed
your cold explanation.

Freezing me into silence
searching for your eyes
riveted on a point
beyond my shoulder.

Leaving me alone
to choose
the sound or
touch.

KID'S STUFF

Take an arm
in both hands
twist in opposite
directions. A
childhood torture
taught early.

Lately

I remember that.

The dawn says,
"give me your
arm".

SEA TURTLES

Sea turtles
lumbering on sand
haunt my dreams.
Peculiar curious
specimens
impressionist fragment
inching through
ocean fog.

Sheltered
in the valley
of the Fox
River, tidy
and swift,
the only turtles
I have ever seen
for fifteen cents
have flowers painted
on their backs.

In dreams
the river swollen
is the sea.
The flowers gone,
tin pie plates will
not hold these
creatures, large
and dark and moving,
lumbering
lumbering
lumbering.

PASSING THE NEIGHBORHOOD MANSION

Who opens the gate?

Children small enough
squeeze through the
twisted wrought iron
fence.

From the steamy sidewalk
the gate appears to
shelter paradise.
Cool trees, more flowers
than anyone could afford
to buy.

I squeezed through
once -- but once
the fence was at
my back the
vast green lawn
was more forbidding
than the fence
had been.

I scrambled back.

I biked hot
summer sidewalks;
rushing breezes
whipped an arrogant disdain.
Those years I never
saw the gate.

Sometimes now
as I slowly make
my way through
sidewalk crowds
guiding your chair
I pause before
the gate to rest.

Who opens the gate?

It's all electronic
now, I suspect,
which sets me to
thinking, maybe
next year I'll be able
to afford
a motorized chair.

ONLY WHERE THE BUS GOES

The bus station
is new.
I wandered in to
warm myself
on a raw day.

Crowded with strangers
searching for others,
I was caught by stares,
released, of no
consequence.

Thawing
I considered a ticket.
I never travel on buses,
no need.

My life is circumscribed
by tight boundaries.
School, stores I reach
by car.
For exercise I circle
the same nine blocks.

I could go just
for fun but,
a bus is slow;
the route proscribed.

Too warm
I'll walk for now
bounded by my choices.
I do not want to go
only where the bus goes.

TOPAZ

I found
a tiny topaz
among the costume
jewelry
left by Mother.
Color of sun
on a summer morning.

It was not her style.
She wore heavy
gold, amber beads,
turquoise reminders
of trips west.

Her last days
pain, joking through
cracked lips,
"does anyone leave
here feet first"
heart monitor
flat
her patch had slipped
more pain.

Those days remain
between her life
and mine.

I never saw her wear
the topaz.
A lover's gift perhaps?

I'll give the other
jewelry
to the grandkids
to remind them.

I'll keep the topaz,
color of sun
on a summer morning.

WITHOUT A NET

In winter
I need to settle for
flowers on fabric
palm trees on T.V.
the memory of
warm sand.

The circle of safety
grows smaller.
Mother is a memory.
My daughters
are the mothers now.

I stand accused
of wisdom
only this
living what remains
without a net.

I'M STANDING ON MY TOES AGAIN

I'm standing
on my toes again
wishing
I were taller.

When I was eight
I climbed
a metal ladder to the
roof tops of Kenosha,
jumped like Errol Flynn
from roof to roof,
a skinny little
girl believing
she could make it,
and I did
until my Poppa
called the cops
who rescued me and
said, "you might have
fallen."

Head hung
in shame
because I'd worried
them, I whispered,
"but I didn't".